BRIGHT FUTURES: AN ANALYSIS OF INDIA'S RIGHT TO EDUCATION ACT

AVANI LANKAPALLI

Contents

Author's Note

In this book, I take you through the journey of first, the historical background of India's Right to Education Act and its purpose, followed by its degree of success in implementation, a deeper insight into section 12 (1)(c), implications of the pandemic, and finally, its future. The work of other organizations working to support these disadvantaged parents and students is also highlighted. Much of the focus of the book revolves around the effectiveness of the act itself.

Living in India for the past two years has heightened my realizations to the inequalities in access to quality education, which has prompted me to consider and investigate existing policies in place to address them. I hope that through this book, I will also encourage other students to deliberate and think purposefully about this issue. Confident, yet in humility, I believe that I provide thoughtful consideration of the policy and its ability to facilitate meaningful change to the existing disparities within India's educational system.

I

An Overview

"Knowledge is power. Information is liberating. Education is the premise of progress in every society, in every family." —Kofi Annan.

Being educated is perceived to be a form of empowerment, and enables social change by making citizens act more responsibly. Thus, it is an inalienable human right. Unfortunately, the Indian educational system is marred by disparities in access and quality.

While education is universally seen as the driving force of being an equalizer, systematic disparities in India's educational sector further reinforce other existing social and economic inequalities. This is because access to quality education is a powerful tool in pulling people out of the vicious cycle of poverty by equipping children with skills required for gainful employment and economic well-being.

The enforcement of the Right to Education (RTE) Act in 2010 came at a time when people believed that it represented a momentous step in the hundred-year struggle for equitable education. This Act marked a paradigm shift in India's outlook toward education. Before this, of roughly two hundred million children between the ages of 6 to 14, more than half did not complete their eight years of elementary education.

Before moving on to describing the various provisions of the RTE Act, it is important for us to first consider the disparities in the education system to understand the importance of the act.

When further diving into this topic, I learned that the concept of class is so deeply rooted and ingrained in our society - that it is present even in our educational system. Thus, I will begin by examining the presence of class discrimination starting in government schools. In 2014–15, the median expenditure in government schools was 58% of what it was in its Kendria Vidalayas schools (which are government-run schools for bureaucrats in transferable jobs). Even in the classroom, parenteral class plays a large role in how students are treated, affecting the quality of education delivered and in consequence the student's ability to complete their schooling till a certain grade along with their rate of retention.

I would also like to consider the issue of linguistic exclusion. It is saddening that in a country whose beauty also comes from our immense diversity with almost 22 major languages, there has been a steady decline in the number of languages that have been utilized as a medium of formal instruction from 80 in 1981 to almost 34 in 2009. More uncommon languages have been left neglected by governmental institutions, contributing to a sense of alienation and lack of education for certain groups - especially tribal learners, which is an immense cause for concern. Furthermore, the medium of instruction - particularly for the sciences is primarily conveyed in English. Thus, there is an immediate loss of learning in integral and fundamental subject areas, especially in rural areas.

Another significant, and also widely known and often discussed issue in our communities to address is the lack of education for girls. Although steps have been taken to address this issue, many of these do not address systemic causes of the lower performance of girls. This is attributed to poor teacher capacity, inadequate quality of schools, or the training of teachers, which enables a productive learning experience for girls.

The constitution (Eighty-sixth Amendment) Act, in 2002 inserted Article 21 into the Constitution of India to provide for free and compulsory education for all children in the age group of six to fourteen years recognized as a fundamental right. The Right of Children to Free and Compulsory Education or the Right to Education act (2009), more widely known as the RTE act aims at addressing some of these concerns stated above.

This act was brought in with the hopes of revolutionizing the educational system in India to create equity in access for all. It was enacted by the Parliament of India on 4 August 2009 and in effect on 10th April 2010 was essentially brought out with the promise of every child having the right to full-time elementary education of satisfactory and equitable quality in formal school.

Brief History of the Right to Education Act

A rough draft of this bill was composed in 2005, following which it was met with backlash and strong opposition due to the mandatory provision to provide 25% reservation for disadvantaged children in private schools.

What was surprising for me to learn was that it made India one of the 135 countries to have made education a fundamental right for EVERY child. A significant point to note about this act is its promise of delivering quality education. This consequently does raise expectations for educators and administrators in the field to alter their traditional perception of education as children being simply passive receivers of knowledge through conventional learning methods such as rote learning and the usage of textbooks - which is currently the norm at several government schools. In this regard, the Act stipulates that the curriculum should instead provide for 'quality' learning through the process of several activities, exploration, and discovery. Therefore, a change in mindset in terms of the style of learning may be required.

Breaking Down the Act and Its Provisions:

The words 'Right to Education' by themselves are rather powerful and would have at the time, filled many with hope for the promise of equal access to education for all. In the process of moving on to a deeper exploration of this act, it is important to decode and clearly break down the legal provisions and various aspects of it.

To provide a brief and rather broad overview, they mean that it is obligatory for the government to provide free and compulsory education to each and every child up to grade 8 in India, in a neighborhood school within 1km, up to grade 8. There is no liability in fees that a child must pay that could hinder their ability to pursue and complete their elementary education.

The meaning of 'free education' includes the provision of textbooks, uniform items, stationery, and special educational material for children with disabilities (a significant issue as we have identified before) to alleviate the burden of their school expenses.

Another point to note is that it also involves a 25% mandatory reservation of free admission for grade 1 for economically disadvantaged students in private schools. Hence, the regulations extend beyond government schools, which in itself was a major in aiming to provide equal access to quality education.

The words 'compulsory education' are indicative of the duty of governmental and local authorities to monitor, provide, and ensure admission, attendance, and the completion of elementary education by all children in this specified age group.

The Act also lays down a Benchmark Mandate relating to the ratio of the number of children per teacher, which is maintained for each school, rather than just simply existing as an average for the state, district, or block. This is important as it ensures that there is no presence of rural-urban imbalance in teacher postings - which helps address some of the concerns mentioned earlier, given the often absence of teachers in certain schools.

Another aspect of ensuring access to 'quality' education is building and maintaining classrooms, and drinking water facilities (with the aim of closing gaps in infrastructure) and maintaining stipulations for the number of working days and hours. Each primary and middle school in India must comply with this set of norms to maintain this minimum standard which is set by the Right to Education Act. Furthermore, it provides for the appointment of appropriately trained teachers with academic qualifications.

Something that I found rather intriguing is the 'no fail' policy that was set forth. It is mandatory to pass all students up until they reach middle school, regardless of how well they perform in their exams. The intention behind this is to not discourage students more than they already might be, make them excited about learning, and thereby possibly aim to avoid a high dropout rate - which is a common trend among government schools. However, this was later amended to include that if a student were to fail a second time, then they would need to repeat a grade.

Role of Private Institutions

As mentioned earlier, private institutions also have a guideline to follow. To be more specific, Section 12(1)(c) of the Act makes it compulsory for every private unaided school to admit at least 25% of its entry class from children belonging to disadvantaged groups. The government reimburses schools an amount equal to the fees charged must be followed by private institutions as well.

Private institutions are an umbrella term used by the government to categorize international schools, residential schools, schools run by religious charitable trusts, and even those run by NGOs. Respective states, however, are free to make their own rules regarding any documentation and paperwork which might be needed for the admissions process.

II

An Exploration Into the Implementation Process

It is important to consider the degree of success in terms of the implementation of the act to evaluate the extent to which it is enabling strides to be made in the educational sector of the country.

The grave nature of the situation is that RTE failed to recognize and address some of the root causes behind the disparities in the educational system which were discussed earlier. The act has been met with criticism from some due to inadequate amounts of time, expert consultation, and effort that had been involved in the process of drafting it.

Several barriers affect the implementation of RTE, such as the lack of availability of infrastructure, awareness, and participation by state/center governments and private schools. It is now clear that there are still much bigger strides that need to be made, and past actions in this regard to be reconsidered.

Inadequate Infrastructure

According to a 2012 report published by the Right to Education Forum (a network consisting of approximately 10,000 NGOs), 95.2% of the schools were not compliant with RTE infrastructure indicators. Between 2009-2010, merely 4.8% of government schools had all the infrastructure facilities that were required for implementation, where only 4.8% of schools had all the 9 required facilities, and 30% of schools had a complete absence of any of them.

The situation seems rather grim, with 1 in 10 schools lacking basic drinking water facilities, and 40% not having functional toilets and separate toilets for girls. Approximately 3% of children don't have access to primary schools within walking distance in their neighborhood, and thus have to travel long distances which is impractical given their socio-economic condition which gives rise to logistical issues.

These infrastructure issues have been reported to be because of a lack of funding. The concern regarding inadequate infrastructure is further exacerbated by the fact that the quality of education varies widely across the country. This is attributed towards varying levels of funding allocated towards training and other infrastructure.

The caliber of teachers is undoubtedly one of the most integral aspects in ensuring access to a quality educational experience, and thus ultimately paves the way for successful implementation. Good teachers have the ability to inspire students and instill their passion for learning, and therefore it is very unfortunate that many students don't have the opportunity to learn from quality teachers. Almost 10.6 lakh teachers were estimated to require professional training as stipulated by guidelines in RTE. However, as of 2017 according to the Human Resources Development Department- there are 11 lakh unqualified teachers.

This is a rather critical concern in states such as Bihar, Uttar Pradesh, Orissa, Assam, Chhattisgarh, and Jharkhand. Forget having a well-trained teacher - as our country grapples with a severe shortage of teachers, some students don't even have access to a teacher. 41% of schools fail to comply with the teacher-student ratio set forth by the act - and this percentage is alarmingly high at between 78 and 88% in places like Delhi and Bihar.

Lack of Awareness

It is deeply saddening that it was the farthest out of reach of those that needed it the most. Both students and their parents do not recognize this as their right, and one that they are certainly entitled to. Between the years of 2016-2018, approximately 200 schools in Rural Pune did not receive even a single application under RTE. Experts also claim that in the state of Maharashtra, almost 50% are vacant.

Examining Implications of the No Fail Policy

As explained earlier, a 'no fail' policy was included to prevent students from having to face the social stigma and fear of failing, one that can be very discouraging to both students and their parents, making them more hesitant to send their kids to school. However, due to inadequate teacher training, most schools were unable to adjust to the new Continuous Comprehensive Evaluation (CCE) style of assessment mandated under RTE, hindering the ability of students to progress.

As some of us might have observed, students from these backgrounds are not necessarily studying in grades that correspond to their age group, especially in their initial years of joining the school. Thus, they follow a rather non-traditional path which would necessitate different accommodations in terms of making sure that their assessment is not based on their age group (which is the current status under the act) - but rather in terms of fulfilling various learning outcomes - which would be fairer and offer a more accurate picture of their learning abilities.

Monitoring

It has been widely observed that the focus on implementation thus far has mostly been on purely admission for students - but tends to ignore what comes afterward. Mostly, there has been no focus or monitoring of the achievement of learning outcomes by students, their achievements, and thus the quality of the education itself.

The degree of success in monitoring the enforcement of guidelines by both private and public schools is limited by low levels of transparency in this process. There is no standardized portal that can be utilized across states that updates stakeholders regarding the progress of students or the number of spots available in each school. Therefore, there is no way to measure the impact made by RTE or check and thus check whether the stipulated norms have been abided, rendering the process of monitoring rather effective.

EPW,2021

Mindset towards the Public Educational Sector

The biggest obstacle to successful implementation is invisible. There has been a widespread, yet unacknowledged, disregard towards the public education system in our society. Hence, there has been a sense of ignorance and lack of effort taken towards allocating funds and improving infrastructure and teachers, being a potential explanation for the rapidly deteriorating quality of the same. Government officials, the general public, and other experts in the field need to alter their perception about public schools and start viewing them as integral common access resources which need to be valued.

Putting The Situation into Scale

Year	No. of students enrolled in class VI-VIII (upper primary)	Year-on-year increase (in %)
2007-08	50,911,110	NA
2009-10	54,467,415	6.5
2011-12	61,955,154	12
2013-14	66,471,219	6.8
2015-16	67,593,727	1.7

Yearly Percentage Increase in Enrollment Levels for Primary School Students (District Information System of Education, 2022)

YEAR	All Management		Government Management	
	Primary	*Upper Primary*	*Primary*	*Upper Primary*
2015–16	84.21	70.70	77.59	52.00
2014–15	83.74	67.38	73.75	48.46

Retention Rates (Unified District Information System for Education, 2022)

Table 3: Percentage of seats filled nationally under section 12(1)(c)

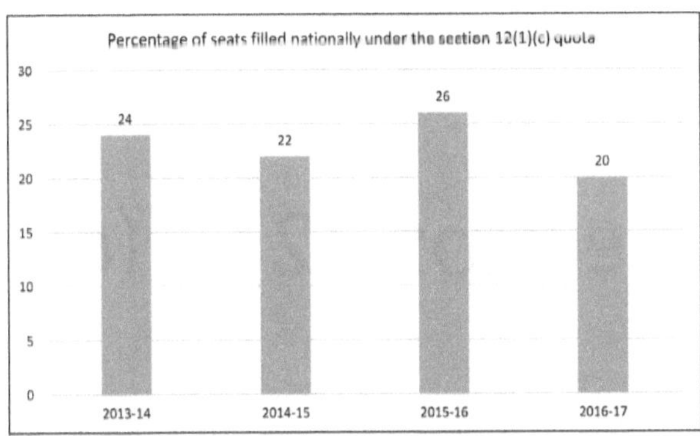

Source: The Bright Spots: Status of Social inclusion through RTE Section 12(1)(c) 2018, Indus Action

Indus Action, 2018

III

Section 12 (1) (c)

As mentioned earlier, private schools have been given a role to play in a section of the act known as RTE 12 (1) (c). This section mandates that 25% of seats in elementary grades in private schools must be reserved for economically disadvantaged students. Thus, through this provision, private schools essentially share responsibility for expanding access to quality education.

This part of the act has over the past couple of years emerged as a significant point of contention for educators, public policy officials, administrators, and even parents. Some believe that the government shouldn't interfere in the workings of the private educational sector, while others believe that since the quality of public schools is arguably nowhere close to the standard of private schools, this could be a very effective way to provide students from lower-economic backgrounds access to quality education.

This section aims to enable access to english-medium schools without high fees and large distances from their homes acting as a barrier. Research has shown that however, overall, the trend is that the relatively more educated the household, the increased likelihood that they will take advantage of this provision.

This particular section has unfortunately not fulfilled the intended aims which is due to poor implementation, attributed partly because of a lack of cooperation between private schools and public officials along with issues related to miscommunication and a lack of cohesion. The process of getting a low-income student into these schools is extremely tedious and complicated with various steps along the way each with its own challenges.

In a cycle that usually starts with a private school declaring the number of seats and potentially ends with a child entering the school - there are challenges every step of the way that prevents the child from receiving the education that they deserve. As explained earlier, one of the provisions of the act was to set aside 25% of the occupancy for children in economically weaker, scheduled caste(SC) or other backward caste(OBC) backgrounds.

Therefore, the first step for schools is to declare their total number of seats - which nowadays is usually done through a portal. In the years that the act was first introduced, portals were not available, making this process more tedious and rather ineffective - as it would take days to complete.

The next two steps involve a verification process by officers, following which eligible students can then apply for the private schools in the neighborhood. Once again, there are obstacles in this stage as not many students - especially in remote areas, have access to private schools in their locality. Hence, not many states tend to follow this rule. Students who are able to get into the school are entirely by chance by depending on simply a lottery-based system.

If this grueling cycle, filled with endless technicalities was not difficult enough - the real challenge actually starts for students right after they were somehow able to make it through the application stage and the lottery names with selected students are released. Over here - there is resistance from both sides - the parents of the students and the school themselves. On one hand, parents face struggles with the documentation process and have their own inhibitions and doubts about sending their children to schools with unfamiliar backgrounds.

Most parents from these backgrounds fail to understand the true importance of education. Furthermore, they are given very little support - in terms of the filing of grievances - where grievances can take up to almost two years to be addressed. Sometimes, by the time this grievance redressal process is completed, the child has passed the eligible age and is no longer able to obtain what is their right. It is no shock that parents lose patience and consequently their trust in this process. Moreover, oftentimes there is no additional government support when it comes to no extra support provided by the school towards the children to make them feel more comfortable with these circumstances.

This brings me to the next point that we should all be very much aware and conscious of. Sometimes, stigmatization is present from the school's side, where they are reluctant to have students from economically weaker backgrounds to be present in their schools, which means they are not fully welcomed into the community. Therefore, students are discouraged to attend school even if they were able to make it through the application process and somehow get admission. This is important to note as this lack of inclusion for these students is one of the contributing factors that leads to the high drop-out rate, which ultimately contributed to a lower degree of success of the act as a whole.

The overall challenges that have been faced with regards to private schools is that guidelines of the percentage admittance for Economically weaker section (EWS) and Disadvantaged group (DG) categories under the 25% quota is not uniform across states. means that students are susceptible to unfairness and inequalities with regards to whether they are admitted, leading to varying admission rates of these categories across states. On one hand in Madhya Pradesh, 88.2% of seats were filled by these 2 categories whereas in Andhra Pradesh - a mere 0.21% were filled.

In Telangana, for instance, many schools have not abided by the act. This is attributed to the lack of reimbursement by the government as promised which creates a big burden on schools and thus makes it difficult for them to abide by these guidelines. Furthermore, as previously stated, students from these backgrounds face significant discrimination in private schools, with the stigma that they lack the appropriate behaviour to thrive or are a bad influence on other students. As a result, there is a lack of diversity and inclusion in these schools.

This is, however, a two-way street. There is a lack of enthusiasm and even effort by the state governments to implement this in private schools. Experts in the field claim that there has been poor enforcement by the government, with no regulatory board as such present in Telangana for efficient monitoring. Thus, many private schools have reported receiving several fake applications, and even now - over 10 years later schools still lack clarity regarding the rules, which is a contributing factor to the effectiveness and rate of success of the act.

IV

Policy Recommendations

It is imperative now, more than ever, for public-policy makers, leaders in the education system, and even the common citizen to think consciously and commit to bridging the gaps in the implementation of RTE. What we truly need right now are not short-term remedies, but rather comprehensive long-term solutions to combat the issues that plague our education system.

The path forward will certainly not be an easy one, bound to be filled with even more obstacles along the way as seen in the past ten years. I believe that a lot of introspection into the progress made so far is necessary. In the following chapter, I analyze various recommendations made by various stakeholders in the field to hopefully address the crux of the causes of issues that have arisen during the implementation process.

Parents have their hesitancy and lack of awareness and support during the process which hinders their ability to successfully complete the application and thus send their children to school. Moreover, it questions their overall faith in the system and thus ultimately results in their children not taking advantage of the provisions. Thus, swift actions must be taken to fully make parents aware of the processes, and various provisions of the act with clarity.

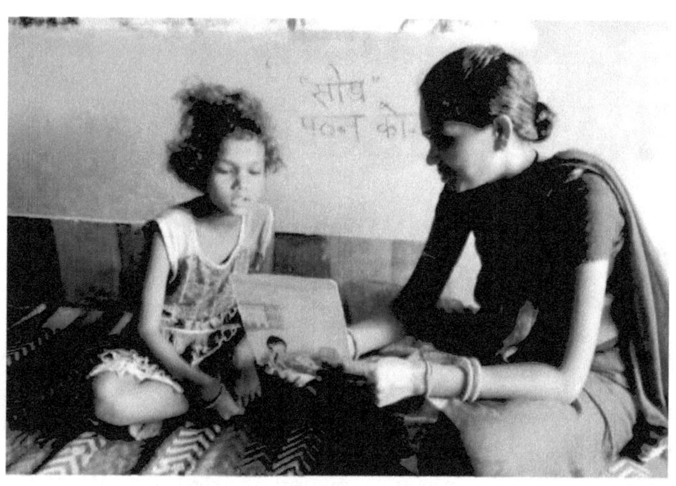

UNICEF, 2022

However, it is important to state that it is certainly not enough to stop simply at the awareness stage. Parents must be provided with sufficient assistance in filling out the forms, to eliminate often overwhelming bureaucratic hurdles that they are very susceptible to.

Large distances deter students from being able to attend school, as mentioned earlier not all students have a school in their neighborhood. Especially for girls, alarmingly high drop-out rates have been attributed to concerns with their safety while traveling. Hence, funds must be allocated or other schemes should be aligned to distribute bicycles and/ or start a school bus system.

System and Database Improvements

Drastic improvements must be made in the grievance redressal system. Increased efficiency in this process would put the parents at more ease and reduce frustration. However, if the system were to be digitized, to increase speed and eliminate the persistent delays, it is also imperative for comprehensive help centers or volunteers(perhaps from the schools themselves) to assist parents who may be unfamiliar with the technology.

Officials and volunteers associated with educational departments working on the ground must be provided with sufficient training to be able to provide support and make sure resolutions for complaints are formulated quickly. Grievances are also one of the ways to address any violations of RTE, and thus are an integral aspect of the monitoring process - which will be explained in further detail later.

Cohesion and coordination are necessary between various agencies to ensure standardization and efficiency as well. This means there must be constant communication between educators, local and nationwide public officials, school administration, school management committees (SMCs), parents, and students. Once again, this reiterates the need for a clear, comprehensive system to ensure monitoring, enforcement, clarity, and thus efficiency. The act initially included guidelines for the creation of SMCs which consisted of parents and other locally elected representatives.

Unfortunately, this did not gain traction with less than 60% of schools as of 2012 having SMCs. There must be more specificity on how to form SMCs - which can be integral in forming relationships between government bodies and schools. Policies can be formulated which can link SMCs to various village plans/schemes which can be crucial in facilitating various district and infrastructure planning processes that are key to more effective implementation.

Co-operation is also necessary between the state and local levels, in terms of implementation of less tangible guidelines such as quality of training for teachers, and evaluation of students. Therefore, the guidelines are left up to the interpretation of local leaders - which inevitably is the cause of the lack of coordination and consistency among key areas between central and state governments. This includes the ministry of women and child development, social justice, labor, education, and tribal affairs - all of which are integral agencies for the successful implementation of RTE.

Monitoring is necessary at every stage and aspect of implementation by different stakeholders. It can be thought of as sort of a central force running through varying parts of the implementation process ensuring quality and the extent to which guidelines stipulated are being followed.

Currently, the act has a rather unique system for monitoring which is done by an entirely separate agency known as the National Commission for Protection of Child Rights (NCPCR). The aim for this - by being separate from the implementing agency can also serve to establish accountability.

However, I would like to note that since RTE is considered a fundamental right, monitoring it can be rather tricky since there is the additional element of taking action to address any violation of this right (CCS). This takes place in the form of complaints and grievances related to any possible violations. Hence, modes for monitoring RTE can be integrated with programs that are included under it.

The District Information System for Education (DISE) can be integrated into the NCPR website which has included report cards and analytical reports for the past five years. These school report cards can be an easy and rather efficient mode of monitoring. Furthermore, it can be linked with the National Commission for protection of Child Rights (NCPR) website to track any violations committed by schools - which can be made visible on this report card. These report cards can include pupil-teacher ratios and other data regarding schools concerning any norms stipulated by the act, and thus the government or a particular school can be held accountable for violation of any of these norms.

RTE can also implement the same format of the Sarva Shiksha Abhiyan(SSA) program - which is aimed at universal education and was introduced before RTE. SSA includes various formats for monitoring the quality of education - and more importantly, it is critically focused on the achievement of learning outcomes.

Now, this is something that the RTE lacks and has faced criticism for. Thus this move can be crucial in improving the learning levels of students. Quality can also be monitored through an indicator developed by UNICEF known as Multiple Indicator Cluster Surveys (MICS) which measure levels of literacy and achievement of learning outcomes (CCS).

However, it is also integral to consider during the monitoring process that non-compliance with any norms must be dealt with on a case-by-case basis. Sometimes schools can't abide by the qualitative norms on RTE - which are infrastructure requirements. For example, in especially schools situated in urban areas, it is impossible to set up a playground given the evident lack of space. In this case, schools should not be penalized or shut down for non-compliance. There is a real risk here of possibly shutting down the only school within the neighborhood that students have access to without considering the reasons behind it, and the ability of a particular school to abide by them. Thus, this may be viewed as a counterproductive practice.

Setting Clear Goals and a Framework for Implementation

Oftentimes, local governments and schools are left without clear-cut goals or a roadmap with what they seek to achieve in terms of the number of students they wish to educate and the learning outcomes they need to fulfill. This ultimately results in poor enforcement and a lack of enthusiasm and effort in its implementation. Thus, both state and central governments must work together to agree on a framework that sets forth clear goals and comprehensive guidelines for implementation relevant to the weaknesses of a specific district, which is backed by constant monitoring, accountability, and transparency.

Change in Focus

Now, it is time for there to be a paradigm shift in the mindset of stakeholders from focusing solely on enrollment, but also on attendance and the retention rates of students. Government schools are believed to have poor retention rates due to poor monitoring and attendance from students. Data finds that the retention rate in an upper primary in 2015-2016 in government schools was 52% compared to a retention rate of 70.70% in private schools. Hence student attendance must strictly be monitored in districts, possibly through the usage of some kind of comprehensive database.

This brings me to my next point - that the fulfillment of learning outcomes for a student must be tracked. A student needs to improve their levels of learning. According to the ASER (Annual Status of Education Report) between 2010 and 2014, reading and mathematics levels nationwide have been more or less stagnant.

This makes the case for educators to endeavor to make improving the actual learning levels for a student a priority. Of course, this again boils down to infrastructure issues and the levels of training for teachers which must be addressed first. However, improving the learning outcomes of students must be a goal that should always be kept in mind during the policy formulation process.

What happens to a child's education after they turn 14?

The mandatory 25% quota on private schools is only up till a child turns 14. It is disturbing to think about the fact that there are many children simply falling through the cracks once they turn 15 with the very real risk of discontinuing education completely beyond this age. Hence, the government must make it a priority to create a state-wide system that monitors students under this quota in private schools and ensures they are mapped towards a public school or allotted a seat elsewhere. However, some might argue that this may still just be a bandaid for a bullet wound. Parents may prefer for their children to drop out and join the labor force instead to support their families.

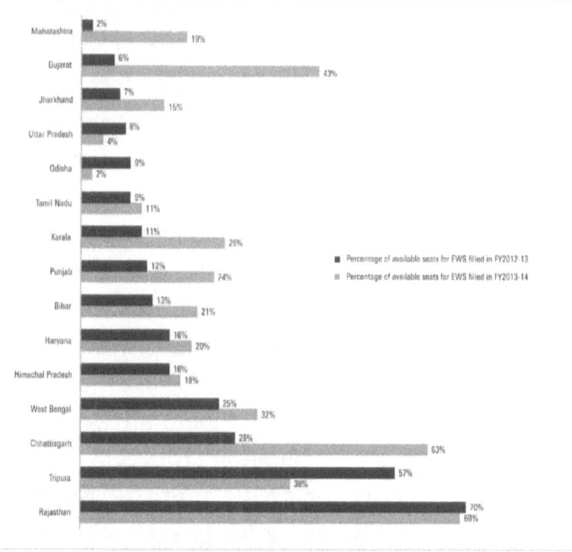

Percentage of Available Seats for Economically Weaker Section (EWS) that has been left vacant (CPR, 2021)

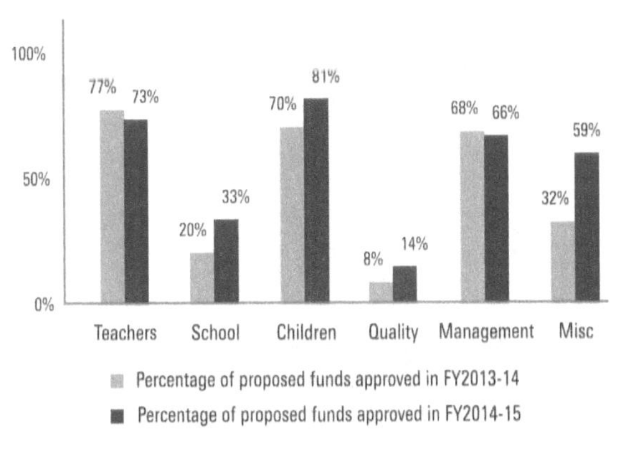

Budget Allocations to Elementary Education (CPR, 2021)

V

Implications of the Pandemic

I would like to conclude the book with a consideration of what the future role of RTE might be following the pandemic.

Nationwide, as of November 2021, approximately 250 million children have been reported to be adversely affected by pandemic-related school closures. India has had one of the longest-duration of school closures in the world. The education systems in our country have sadly borne the brunt of the pandemic, which means that it may be necessary for further reforms in the education sector to make up for these losses which occurred during the dreaded lockdowns and adapt to the newer circumstances. The road to improving implementation is now even more complex.

A significant question to ask is what might become the role of RTE now, and what place does it have in our country in this new environment?

According to an official from the School Education Department, "about one lakh children who got admitted in LKG and UKG in the past two years, did not receive even a single class due to lockdown besides the COVID-19 pandemic situation".

When government schools have struggled to provide even the most basic of infrastructure, it would be out of the question for them to provide access to computers or phones required for the transition to online learning. This is further exacerbated by the poor infrastructure in a student's living environment - such as the lack of a reliable supply of electricity and sometimes the complete absence of wifi facilities. According to a Niti Aayog report, only 23.8% of internet access - with this being a single digit in rural areas. Thus, hoping for a transition to online learning for these demographics would be far out of touch with reality.

Due to the difficulties in providing online educational opportunities for most government schools, many students have fallen through the cracks and dropped out of the system entirely. As a result, the process of tracking students, monitoring, and enforcing has become even more difficult, and some may argue, nearly impossible. Furthermore, to the chagrin of many parents, schools have been forced to halt RTE admissions for nearly three years due to a lack of reimbursements. They have been left stranded with no schooling options for their children. As a result, any progress made in enrollment over the last ten years has been squandered, with reports that the number of out-of-school children has almost doubled during the pandemic.

Nytimes, 2022

A study conducted in Karnataka using household surveys found that in rural areas 33,344 children had dropped out of school by December 2020, and 9716 children had never even enrolled. These findings are rather alarming and put the extent of this situation to scale and perspective. Thus, they demonstrate how the pandemic has completely squandered any progress made in the past couple of years and has led to a rapid deterioration in the learning levels of low-income students.

One might say that the pandemic has exposed the cracks that have been present in our nation's education system, and has further exacerbated them.

The disparities in the education system mentioned before have widened even further. While students from demographics who can afford to attend private schools and access the technology required to facilitate online learning have been able to continue their education, others have completely missed out. This limits any possibility of them moving out of this position and thus has further implications of deepening the vicious cycle of poverty. In effect, it essentially crushes the dreams of millions of families who had hopes of possibly finding better opportunities.

Slow Pace of Vaccination

Vaccination was integral to the smooth reopening processes of all schools. While private schools were able to accomplish this at a relatively fast pace through partnerships with hospitals to complete full vaccination for both parents and teachers, public schools were unable to accomplish this. Thus, the reopening process faced setbacks, further delaying their return to school.

Nytimes, 2022

Nytimes, 2022

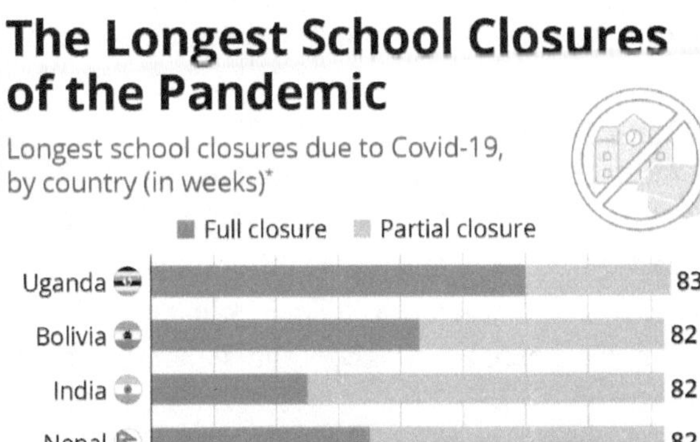

The Longest School Closures of the Pandemic

Longest school closures due to Covid-19, by country (in weeks)[*]

UNESCO, 2022

Mindset on the Importance of Education Worsened?

It would be fair to assume that parents are potentially even more reluctant to send their children to school now. Education has become even less of a priority with skyrocketing unemployment rates over the past two years. Many students have dropped out with no other option left with their families dealing with extreme income losses and COVID-related deaths.

Now, in our return to normalcy, immediate actions must be taken to make up for the major losses in learning in the past 2 and a half years.

I believe that any future steps that are taken must work to address the gaps that were present even before the pandemic, but - making up for these sudden and rather dramatic losses must be made the first priority for both public officials, NGOs, and other stakeholders working in the field.

Bridging the Gap

I would like to conclude by discussing the work that is currently being done by other organizations including NGOs and think tanks to support different stakeholders in the process of implementation. Their role has undoubtedly become more crucial now given the setbacks due to the pandemic.

I have been particularly interested in the work of Indus Action - a Think Tank, that I have recently come across. Among other initiatives, it is focused on enabling the access of disadvantaged parents and students to RTE 12 (1) (c). I chose to highlight their work, given its relevance to my earlier discussion regarding the lack of awareness among parents and students about the act itself and the difficulties faced in the application process. Indus Action provides detailed guidance throughout the documentation process, with volunteers working on the ground to ensure this, alleviating the confusion and frustration that is often faced. Support is also ensured in the lengthy grievance redressal process.

Firstly, at the very fundamental level, Indus Action volunteers ensure that those in need are made aware of the act, which once again as mentioned before - is one of the root causes affecting the ineffectiveness of the policy. To put their impact in more quantifiable terms, with their support, approximately 2.4 lakh students from disadvantaged backgrounds have been admitted to private schools under RTE 12 (1) (c), and more importantly - with an 81% retention rate.

I believe their vision to "bridge the gap between law and action" is powerful because it is a central theme underlying my discussion regarding the implementation of RTE and more specifically the various factors that may be diminishing its effectiveness.

I hope that by prompting a thoughtful consideration of the policy, I have given you the chance to introspect regarding not only the effectiveness of the policy - but the issues faced by millions of children across India in their struggle for education.

References

V. A. P. B. G. (2022, February 22). RTE Act 2009 — Issues and Challenges. Issues and Challenges in India. Retrieved October 21, 2022, from https://socialissuesindia.wordpress.com/2020/07/17/rte-act-2009-anomalies-and-challenges/

Alexander, S. (2019, September 17). How RTE improves access to private schools | Mint. Mint. Retrieved October 21, 2022, from https://www.livemint.com/education/news/how-rte-improves-access-to-private-schools-1568712555594.html

Anjela Taneja. (2020, June 29). How can India's education system escape the vicious cycle of inequality and discrimination? Oxfam India(OIN). Retrieved October 21, 2022, from https://www.oxfamindia.org/blog/how-can-indias-education-system-escape-vicious-cycle-inequality-and-discrimination

Ankur Sarin, Ambrish Dongre, and Shrikant Wad, State of the Nation: RTE Section 12(1)(c), (Ahmedabad: IIM Ahmedabad, 2017), accessed 31 July 2019, https://cprindia.org/ system/tdf/policy-briefs/ SOTN%20Report%202017_FINAL.pdf?file=1&type=node&id=

Arora, N. (2020, September 11). India's Right to Education is failing in reality – The Leaflet. The Leaflet – an Independent Platform for Cutting-edge, Progressive, Legal, and Political Opinion. Retrieved October 21, 2022, from https://theleaflet.in/indias-right-to-education-is-a-failing-in-reality/

Arora, K., Yadav, N., Madan, S., & Abhishek, S. (2017). Evaluating section 12 (1)(C) of right to education (RTE) in Delhi. ZENITH International Journal of Business

Economics & Management Research, 7(12), 24-35.

Assessing the impact of Right to Education Act. (2016, March). KPMG. https://assets.kpmg/content/dam/kpmg/pdf/2016/03/Assessing-the-impact-of-Right-to-Education-Act.pdf

Batra, P. (2017, August 29). RTE amendment giving teachers more time to get qualified is poorly thought out and contrary to law. Scroll.in. Retrieved October 21, 2022, from https://scroll.in/article/847310/rte-amendment-giving-teachers-more-time-to-get-qualified-is-poorly-thought-out-and-contrary-to-law

Bedi, A. (2015, November 19). Lack of infrastructure at Rly Colony govt school makes mockery of RTE. Hindustan Times. Retrieved October 22, 2022, from https://www.hindustantimes.com/punjab/lack-of-infrastructure-at-rly-colony-govt-school-makes-mockery-of-rte/story-hY6puXMbp4lkPJeokkbd4O.html

Bhalla, V. (2021, April 12). Education, a casualty in the pandemic violating rights of students – The Leaflet. The Leaflet – an Independent Platform for Cutting-edge, Progressive, Legal, and Political Opinion. Retrieved October 21, 2022, from https://theleaflet.in/education-a-casualty-in-the-pandemic-violating-rights-of-students/

Bhattacharjee, S. (2019). Ten years of RTE Act: Revisiting achievements and examining gaps. ORF Issue Brief.

Correspondent, D. (2022, March 15). Private schools give a damn to admissions under RTE Act. Deccan Chronicle. Retrieved October 21, 2022, from https://www.deccanchronicle.com/jobs-education/150322/private-schools-give-a-damn-to-admissions-under-rte-act.html

Desk, I. T. W. (2021, December 1). Right to Education Act: Significance, guarantees, gaps and reforms. India Today.

Retrieved October 21, 2022, from https://www.indiatoday.in/education-today/gk-&-current-affairs/story/right-to-education-act-significance-guarantees-gaps-and-reforms-1883012-2021-12-01

Engaging parents to overcome reading poverty (India). (n.d.). UNICEF. Retrieved October 21, 2022, from https://www.unicef.org/documents/engaging-parents-overcome-reading-poverty-india

Ghosh, L. (2012, April 18). What are the challenges & possible solutions in the implemention of RTE Act. The Economic Times. Retrieved October 21, 2022, from https://economictimes.indiatimes.com/industry/services/education/what-are-the-challenges-possible-solutions-in-the-implemention-of-rte-act/articleshow/12697894.cms?from=mdr

Indus Action. (2022). Indus Action – Bridges the gap between Law & Action. Retrieved October 22, 2022, from https://www.indusaction.org/

Jha, P., & Parvati, P. (2014). Assessing progress on universal elementary education in India: A note on some key constraints. Economic and Political Weekly, 44-51.Jolad, S. (2015, August 19). Five Suggestions For The New Education Policy. Swarajyamag. Retrieved October 21, 2022, from https://swarajyamag.com/books/five-suggestions-for-the-new-education-policy

Joshi, P. (2018, March 30). Awareness about RTE in rural areas very low. The Bridge Chronicle. Retrieved October 21, 2022, from https://www.thebridgechronicle.com/pune/awareness-about-rte-rural-areas-very-low-15597

Kapur, N. (2020, January 14). From Reorganization Of J&K To CAA: 5 Controversial Acts Of 2019. Youth Ki Awaaz. Retrieved October 21, 2022, from https://www.youthkiawaaz.com/2019/12/five-acts-passed-in-2019-that-garnered-the-most-attention-of-indian-public/

Kaushal, M. (2012). Implementation of Right to Education in India: Issues and Concerns. Journal of Management & Public Policy, 4(1).

Lafleur, M., & Srivastava, P. (2019). Children's accounts of labelling and stigmatization in private schools in Delhi, India and the Right to Education Act. Education Policy Analysis Archives, 27, 135-135.

Vijay Kutty/IndiaPictures/Universal Images Group via Getty Images. (2022, October 21). India At 73: Milestones That Made Us | Page 4. Forbes India. Retrieved October 22, 2022, from https://www.forbesindia.com/aperture/slideshow/india-at-73-milestones-that-made-us/61691/4

Mehta, S. (2021, November 11). Education In India During Covid-19: Challenges Faced And Solutions For A Post-Pandemic Era. https://www.outlookindia.com/. Retrieved October 21, 2022, from https://www.outlookindia.com/website/story/opinion-education-in-india-during-covid-19-challenges-faced-and-solutions-for-a-post-pandemic-era/400485

Mondal, M. A. (2015). A study on the Awareness about the RTE Act, 2009 among teachers of elementary schools in West Bengal. GHG Journal of Sixth Thought, 2(1), 1-4.

Nic, L. P. (n.d.). Right to Education | Ministry of Education, GoI. Retrieved October 21, 2022, from https://dsel.education.gov.in/rte

nytimes.com. (2022, January 27). Retrieved October 22, 2022, from https://www.nytimes.com/2022/01/27/world/asia/india-schools.html

No water, no toilet: 95% schools in India lack RTE infrastructure-India News ,. (2012, April 8). Firstpost. Retrieved October 21, 2022, from https://www.firstpost.com/india/no-water-no-

toilet-95-schools-in-india-lack-rte-
infrastructure-269363.html

Paik, S. (2022, May 30). Less than 20% of students in India could access education in pandemic, learning suffered. ThePrint. Retrieved October 21, 2022, from https://theprint.in/pageturner/excerpt/less-than-20-of-students-in-india-could-access-education-in-pandemic-learning-suffered/972901/

Purkayastha, M. (2021b, June 18). Why the Right to Education law hasn't worked wonders. Deccan Herald. Retrieved October 21, 2022, from https://www.deccanherald.com/opinion/panorama/why-the-right-to-education-law-hasnt-worked-wonders-998655.html

Rajamane, R. S. A. M. (n.d.). India Can't Keep Citing the Pandemic to Deprive Children of Education. The Wire. Retrieved October 21, 2022, from https://thewire.in/education/india-cant-keep-citing-the-pandemic-to-deprive-children-of-education

Reddy, S. T. K. N. & B. (2021, September 19). Government schools redeem their popularity among the Telangana middle class. . . The New Indian Express. Retrieved October 21, 2022, from https://www.newindianexpress.com/states/telangana/2021/sep/19/government-schools-redeem-theirpopularity-among-the-telangana-middle-class-2360747.html

Right to Education (RTE) Act: Future of Children. (2022, March 11). Getlegal India. Retrieved October 21, 2022, from https://getlegalindia.com/right-to-education/

RTE Act 2009 — Issues and Challenges. (2022, February 22). Issues and Challenges in India. Retrieved October 21, 2022, from https://socialissuesindia.wordpress.com/2020/07/17/rte-act-2009-anomalies-and-challenges/

Sadam, R. (2021, September 16). Why 1.25 lakh private school students in Telangana moved to govt schools in 2021. ThePrint. Retrieved October 21, 2022, from https://theprint.in/india/education/why-1-25-lakh-private-school-students-in-telangana-moved-to-govt-schools-in-2021/734064/

Sathyanarayana, R. (2022, February 12). Pandemic douses RTE flames of hope. DT Next. Retrieved October 21, 2022, from https://www.dtnext.in/tamilnadu/2022/02/12/pandemic-douses-rte-flames-of-hope

Targetstudy.com. (n.d.). Right to Education | Importance | Provisions | Implementations. Retrieved October 21, 2022, from https://targetstudy.com/articles/right-to-education.html

The Hindu. (2012, April 4). Lack of school infrastructure makes a mockery of RTE. Retrieved October 21, 2022, from https://www.thehindu.com/news/national/lack-of-school-infrastructure-makes-a-mockery-of-rte/article3281720.ece

The Hindu. (2016, December 17). Joining hands in the interest of children. Retrieved October 21, 2022, from https://www.thehindu.com/opinion/lead/Joining-hands-in-the-interest-of-children/article16654695.ece

The Hindu. (2020, March 15). SC, ST student admissions in private schools dismal: Congress. The Hindu. Retrieved October 21, 2022, from https://www.thehindu.com/news/cities/Hyderabad/sc-st-student-admissions-in-private-schools-dismal-cong/article31076540.ece

Thapliyal, N. (2012). Unacknowledged rights and unmet obligations: An analysis of the 2009 Indian Right to Education Act. Asia-Pacific Journal on Human Rights and the Law, 13(1), 65-90.

UDISE+, UDISEPLUS, UDISE, UDISE CODE, School Directory Management, School Data Capture. (n.d.).

REFERENCES

UDISE+. Retrieved October 22, 2022, from https://udiseplus.gov.in/

What's Ailing Primary Education in Rural India: A Case Study of a. (2021, August 15). Economic and Political Weekly. Retrieved October 21, 2022, from https://www.epw.in/engage/article/whats-ailing-primary-education-rural-india-telangana-case-study